Vintage Tea Party
Tea lovers Coloring book for adults

Copyright © 2019 by Color me Vintage

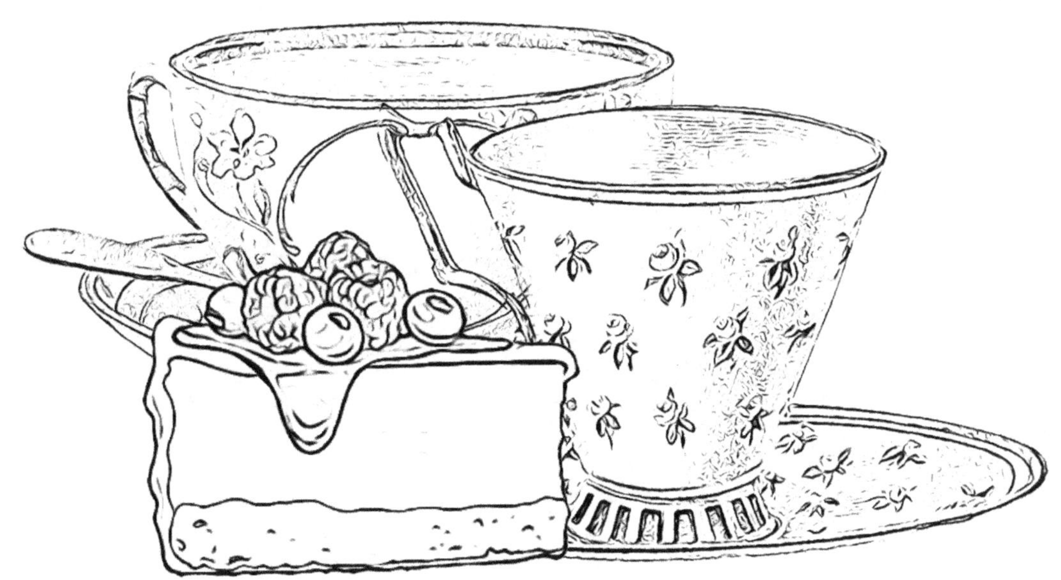

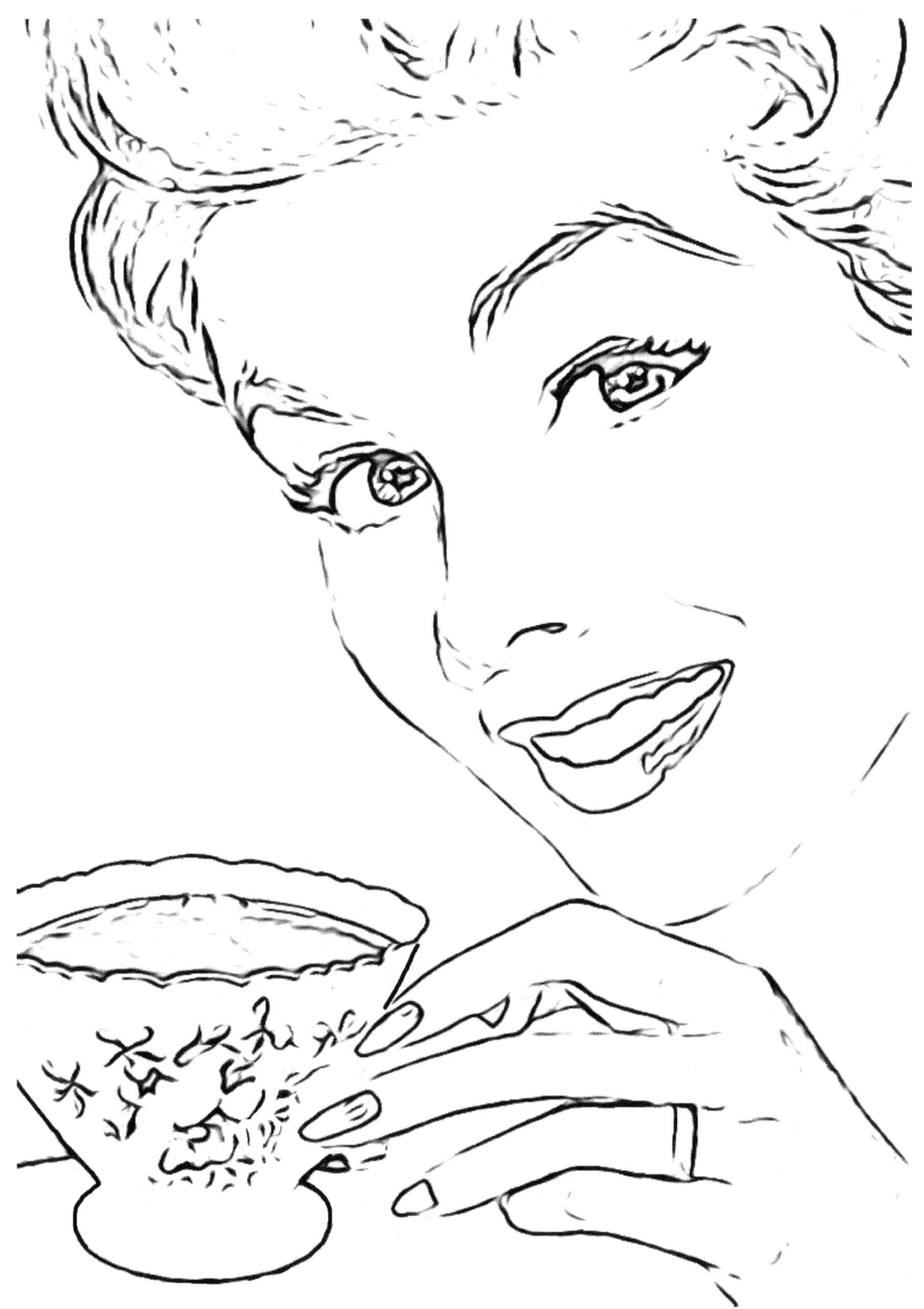

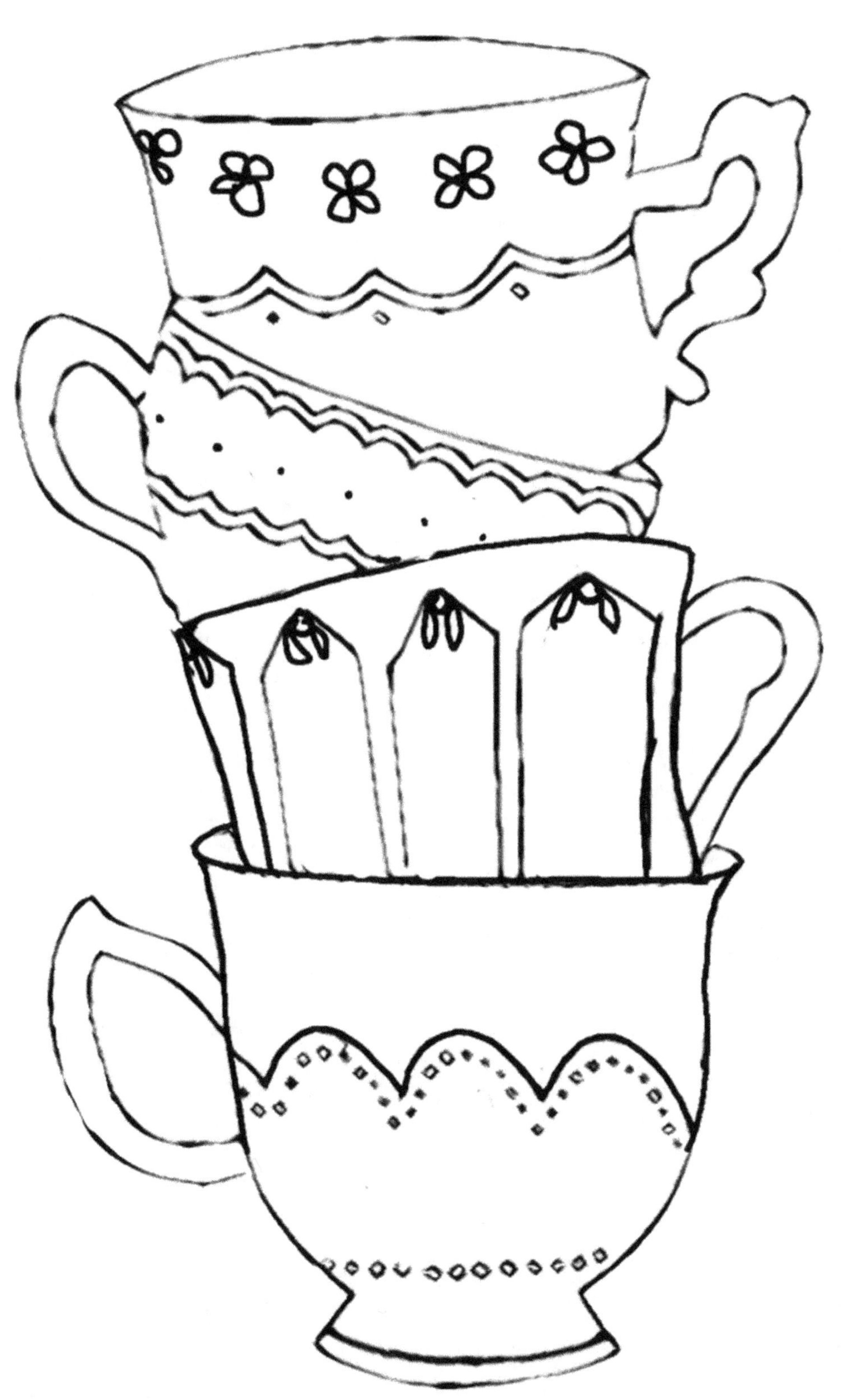

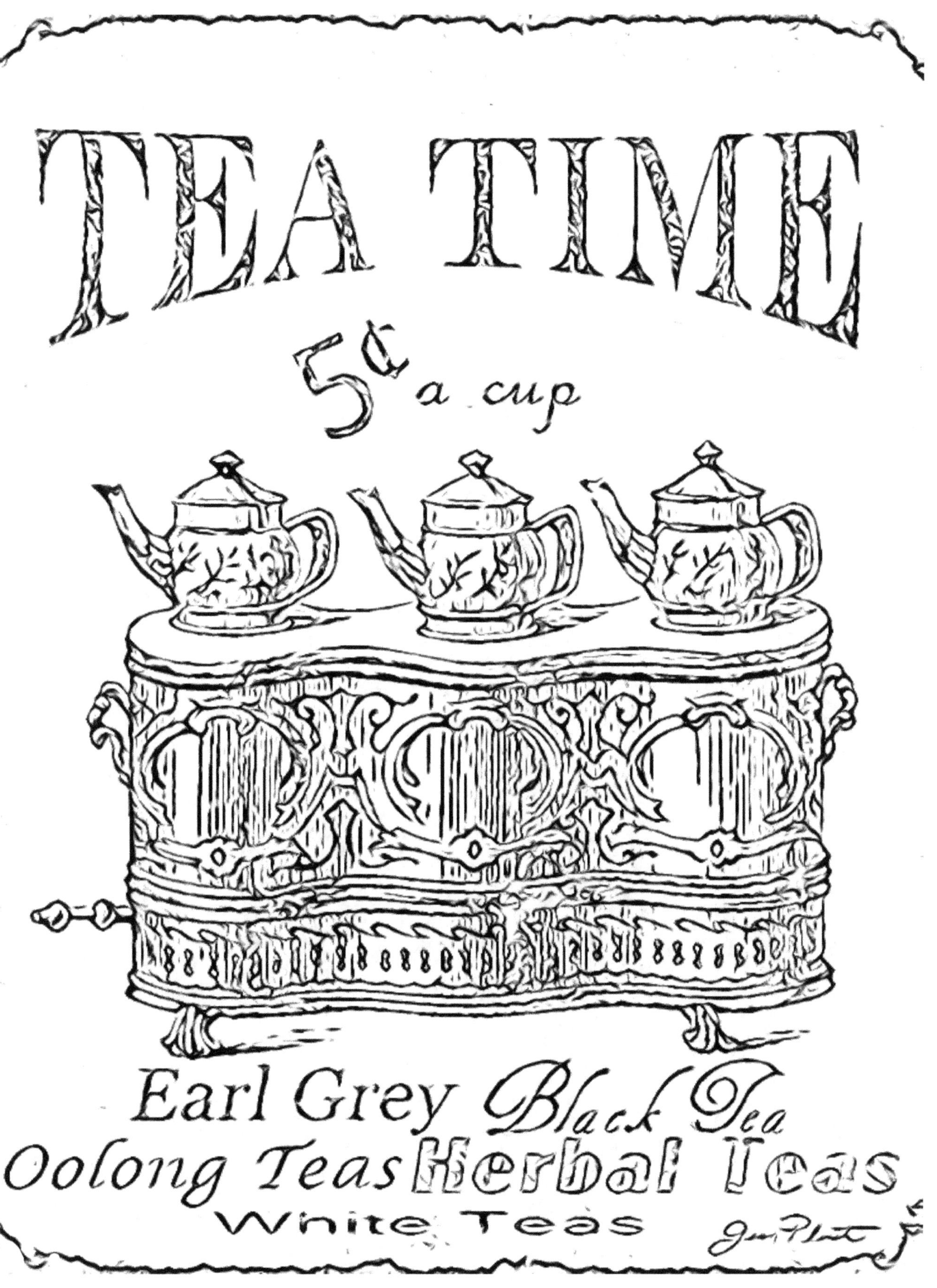

TEA TIME
5¢ a cup
Earl Grey Black Tea
Oolong Teas Herbal Teas
White Teas

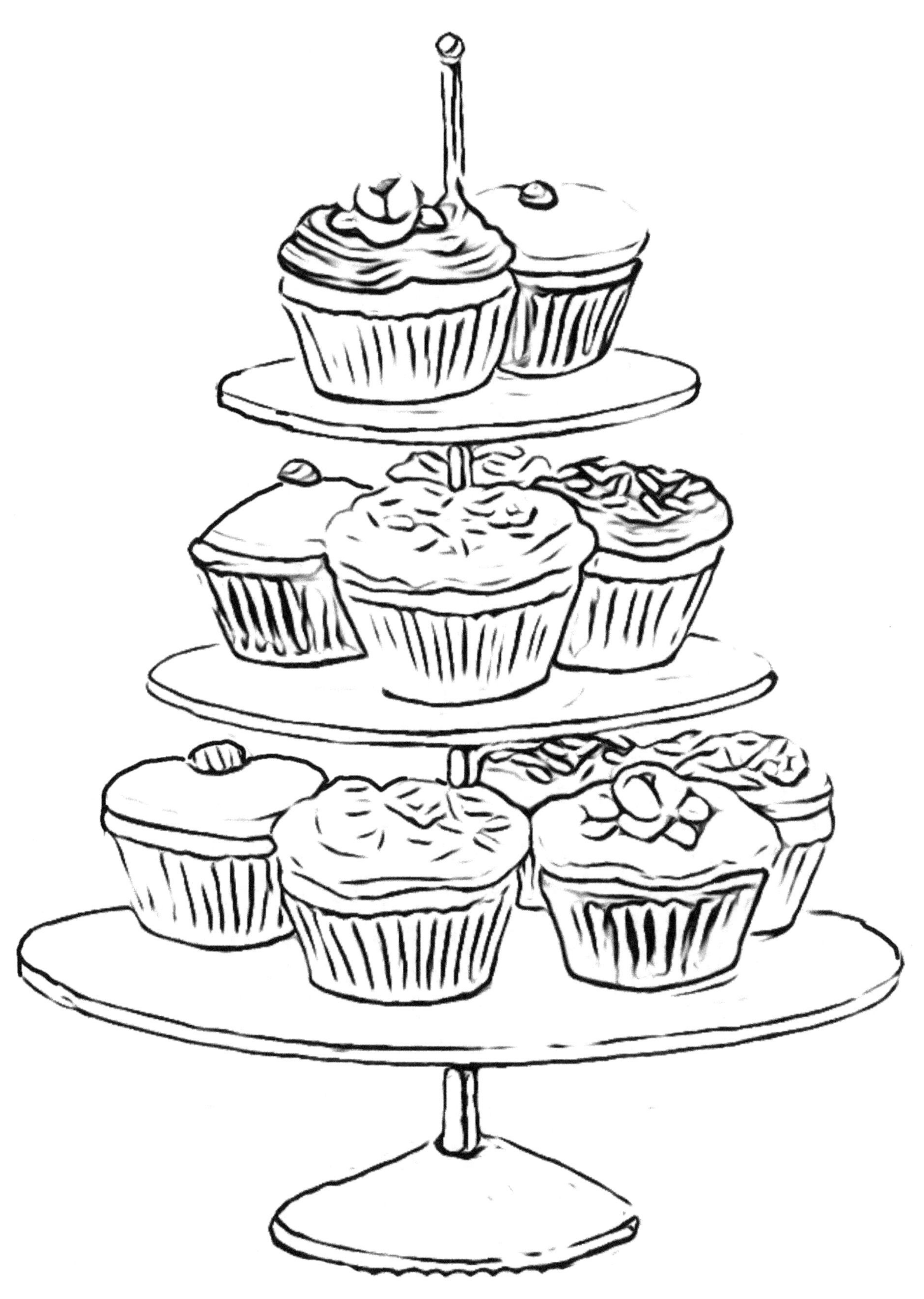

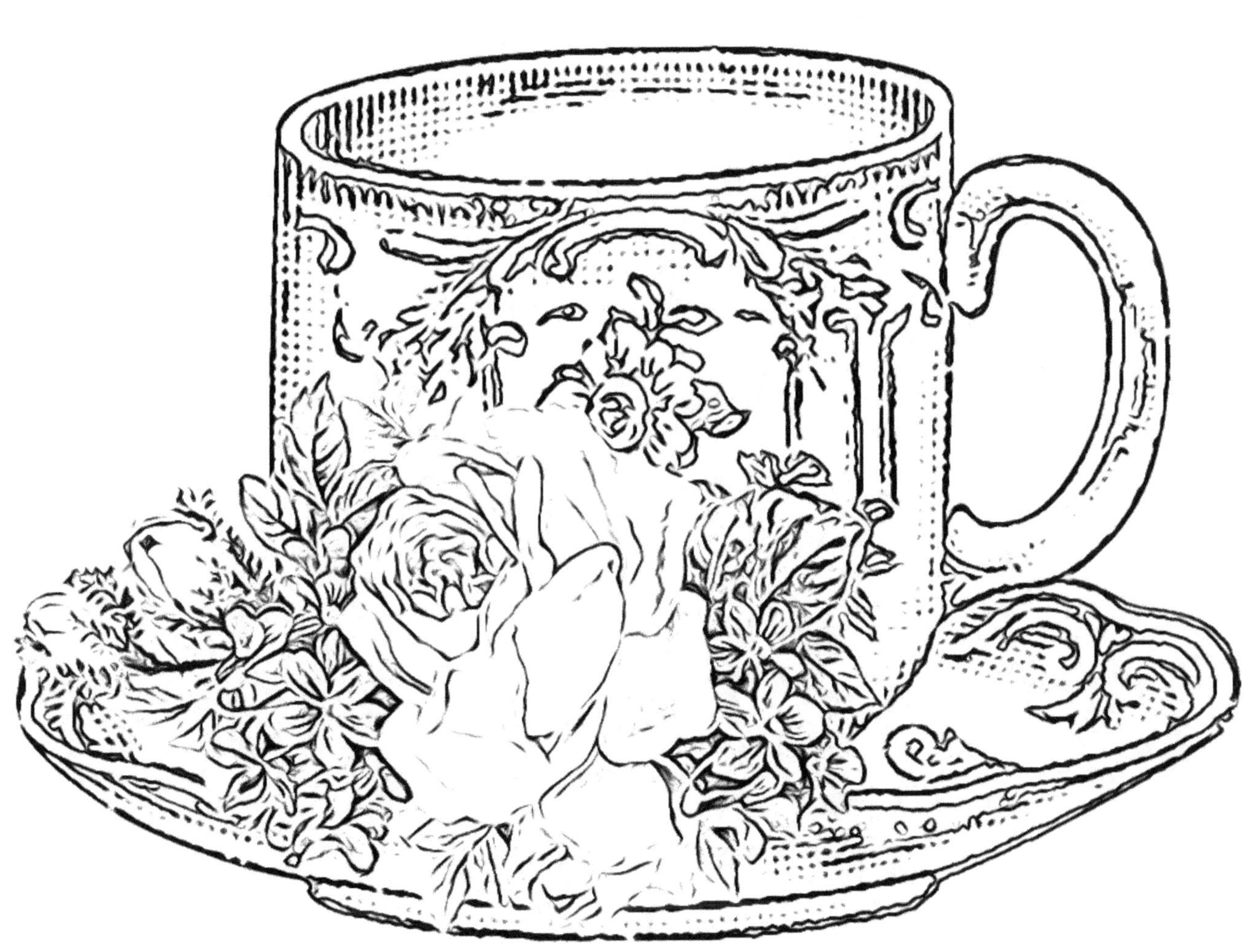

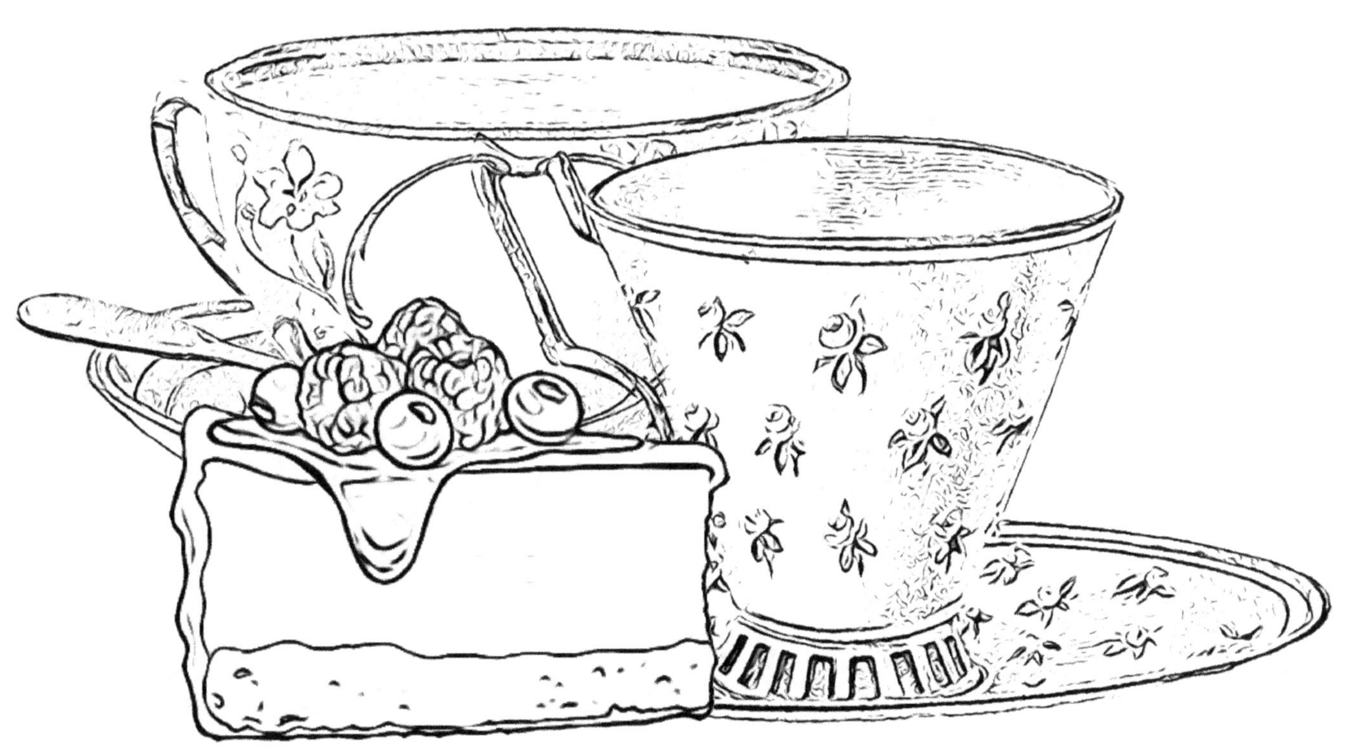

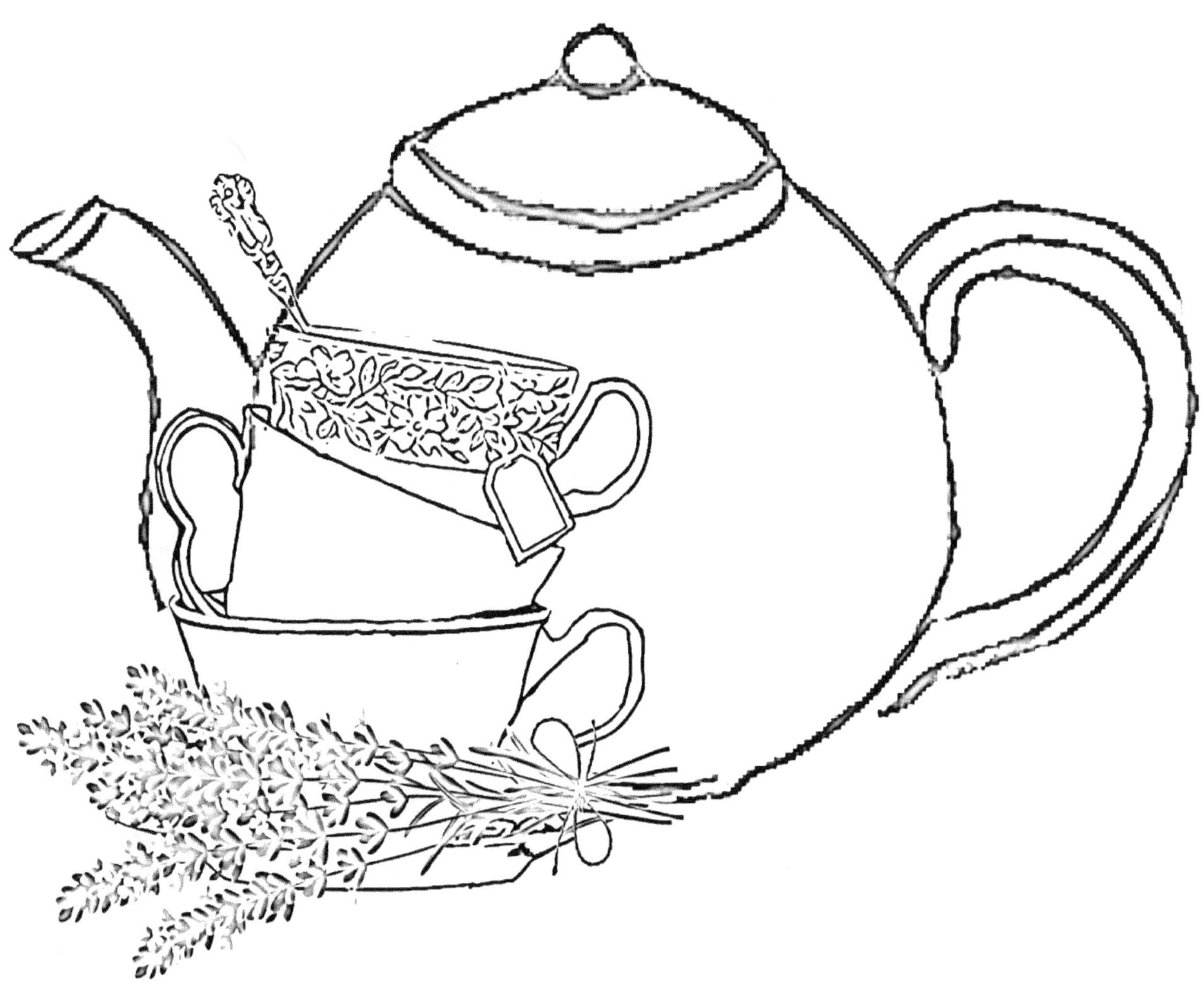

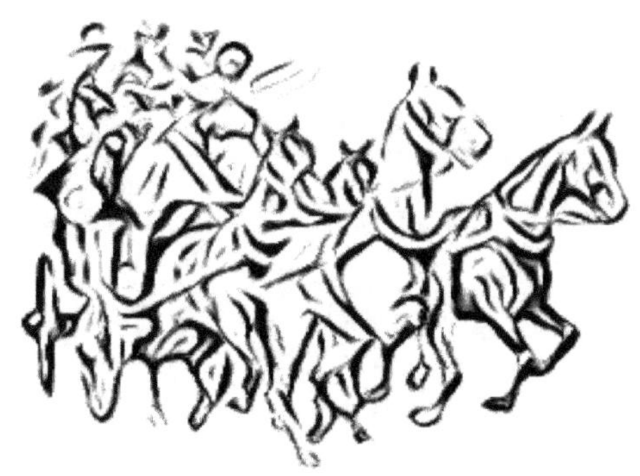

DOUWE EGBERTS

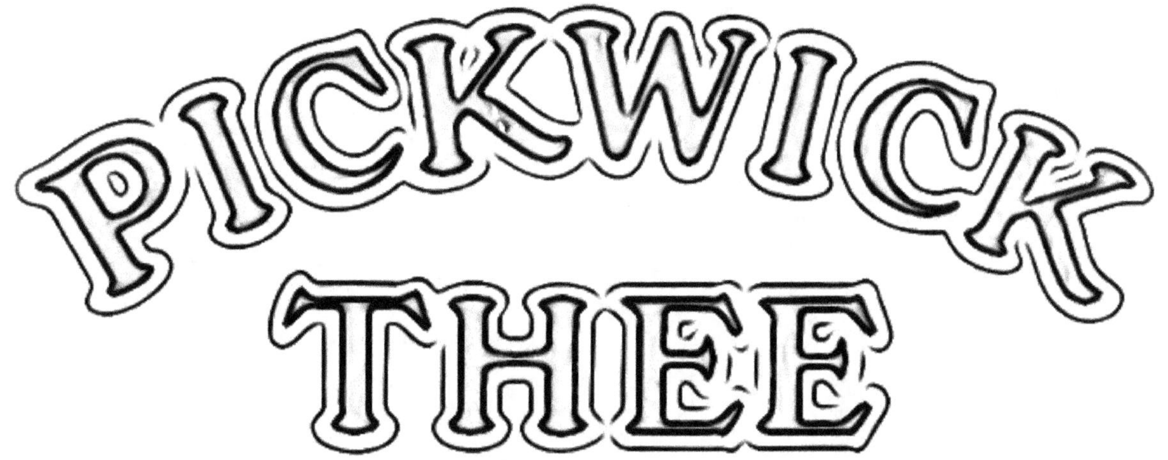

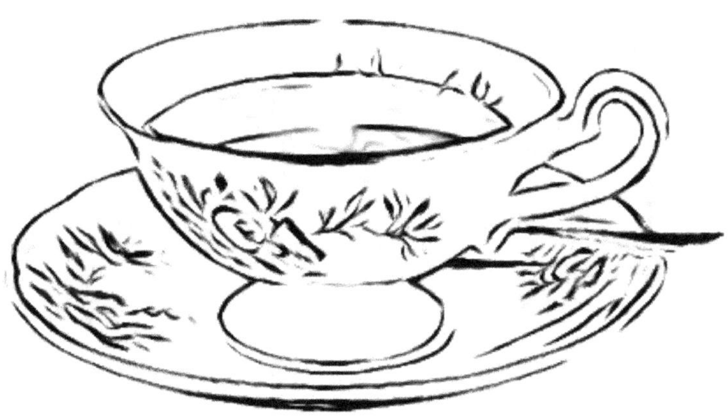

Fijne Engelse Melange

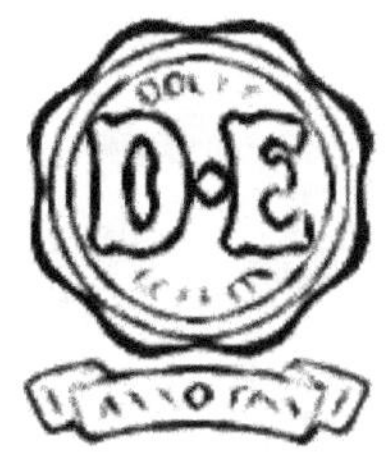

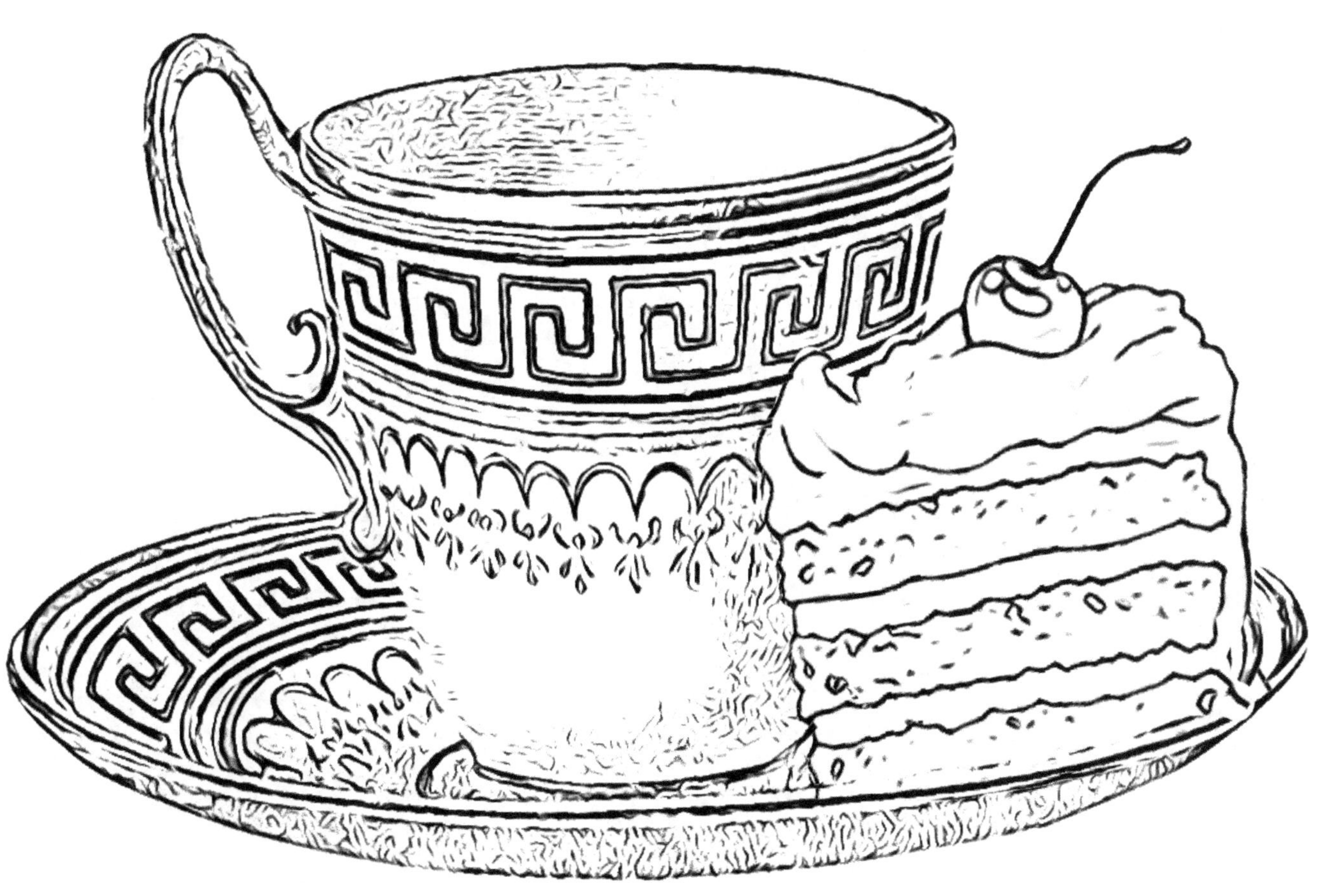

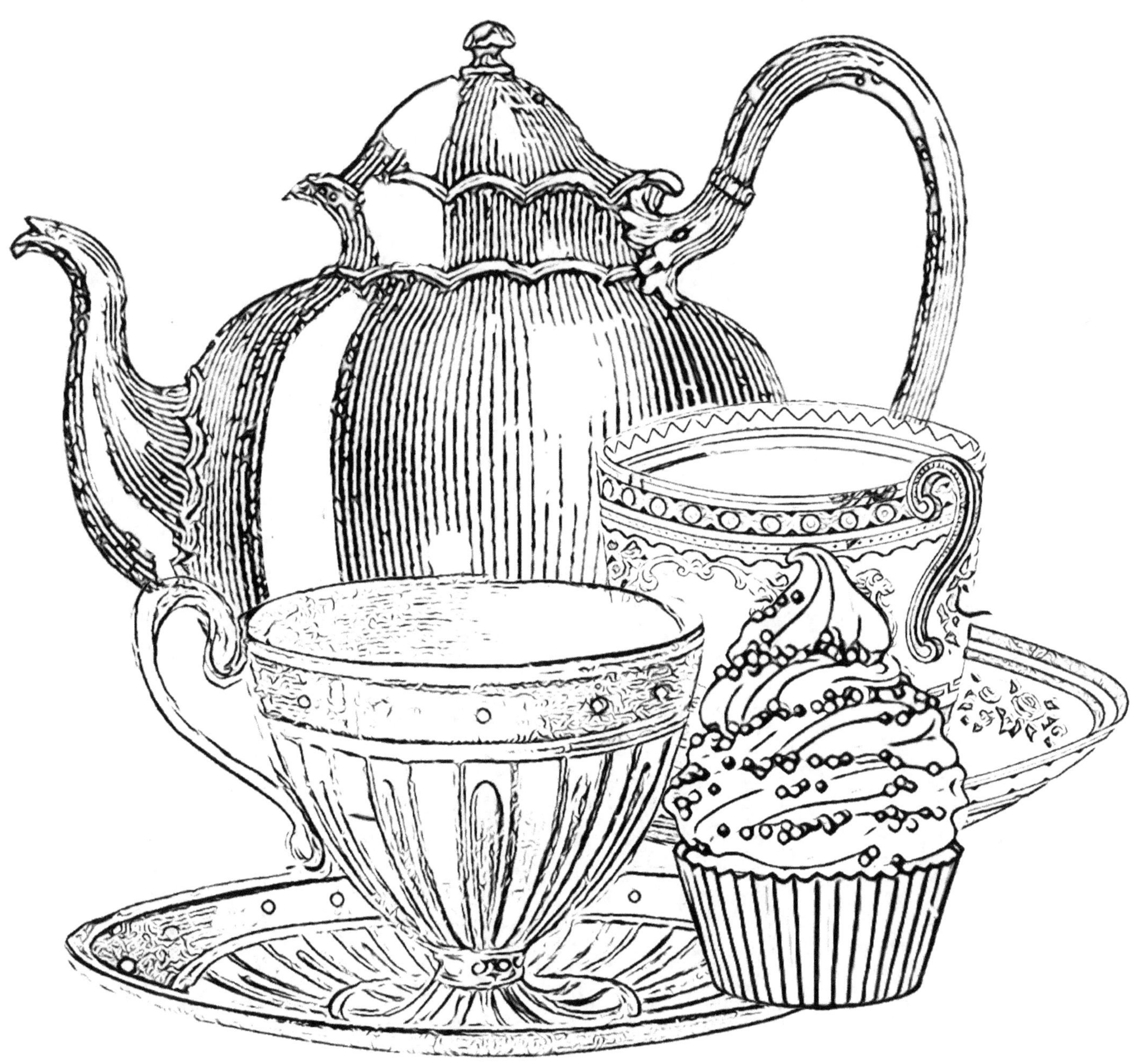

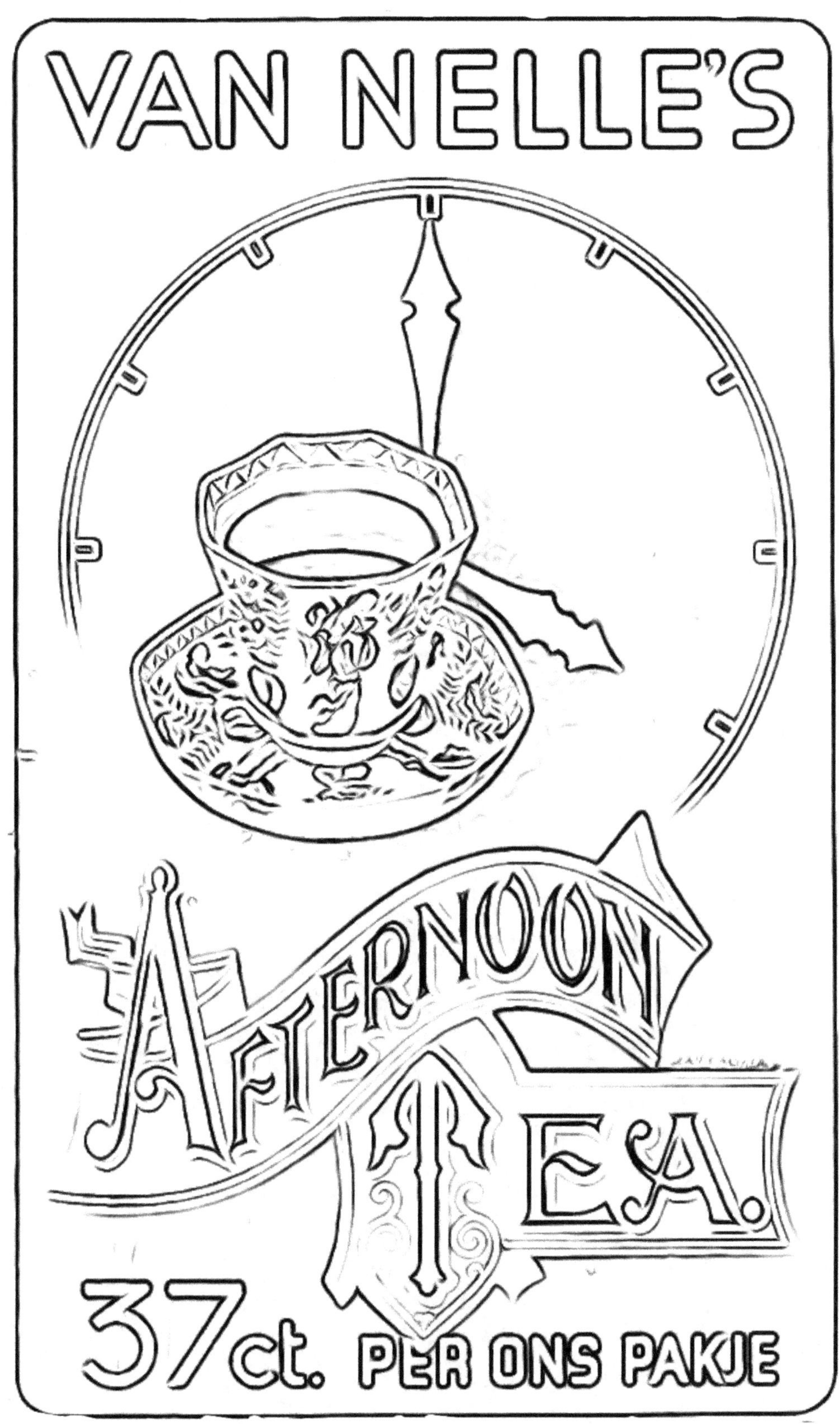

VAN NELLE'S
AFTERNOON TEA
37 ct. PER ONS PAKJE

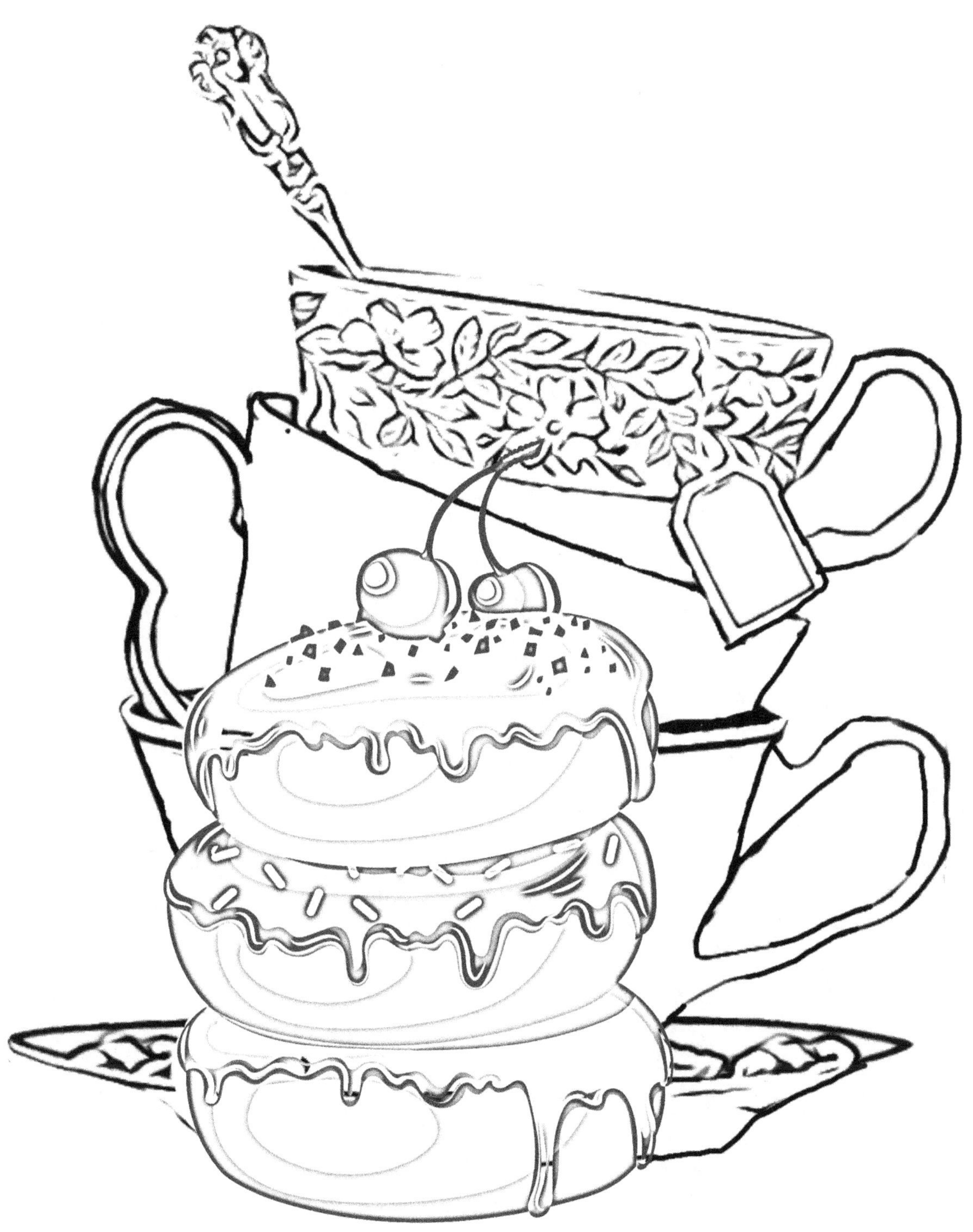

The Great Tea Company

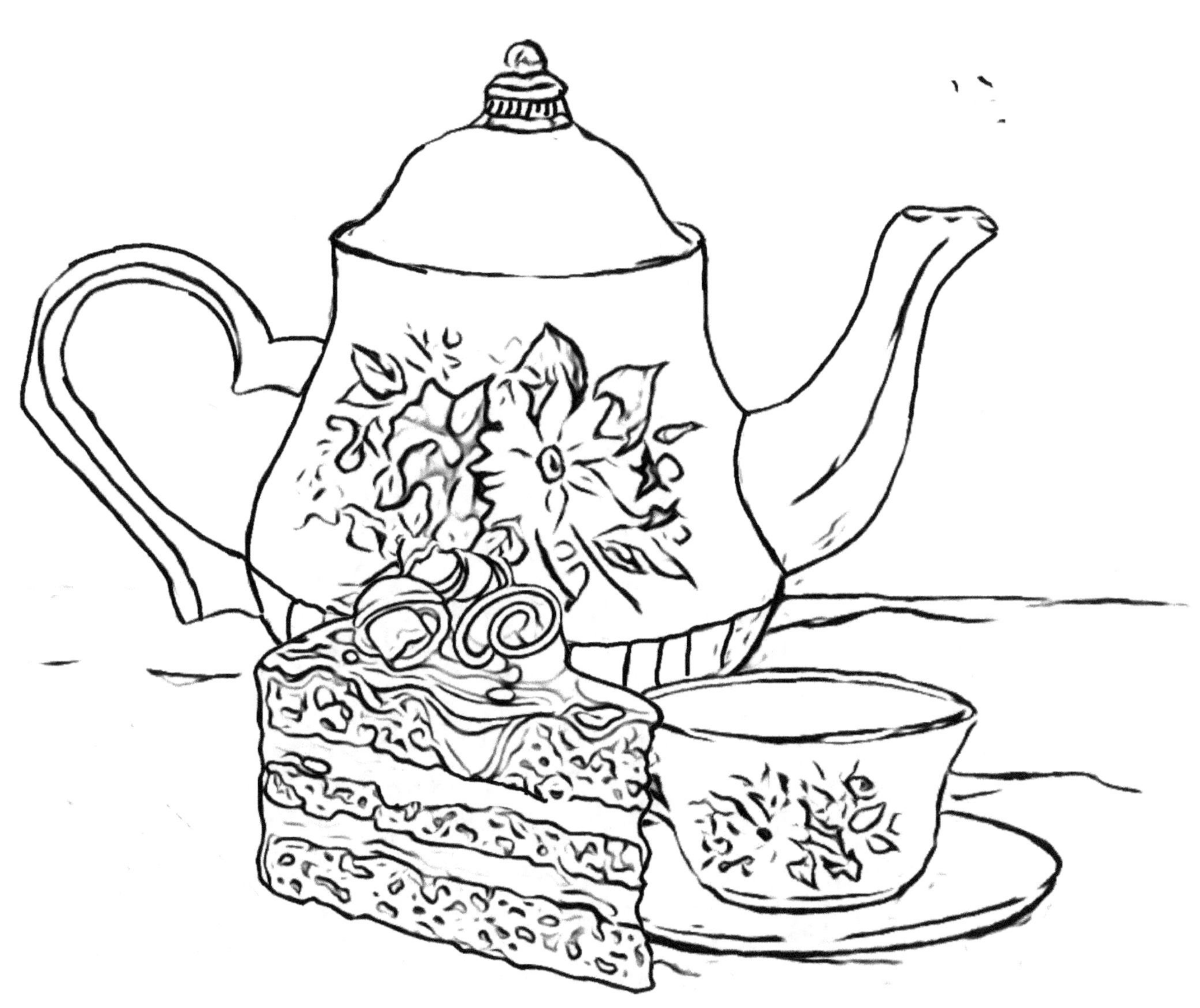

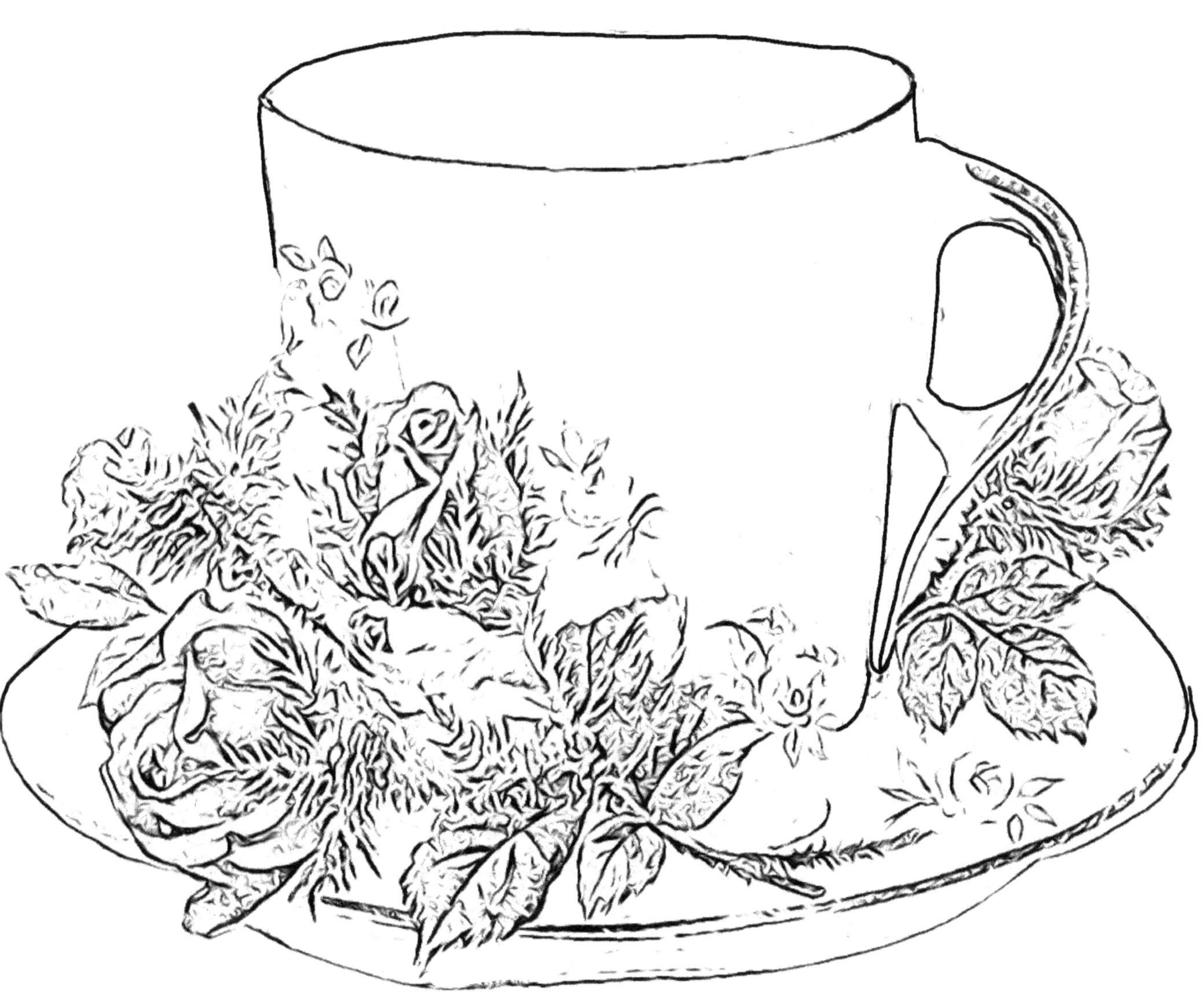

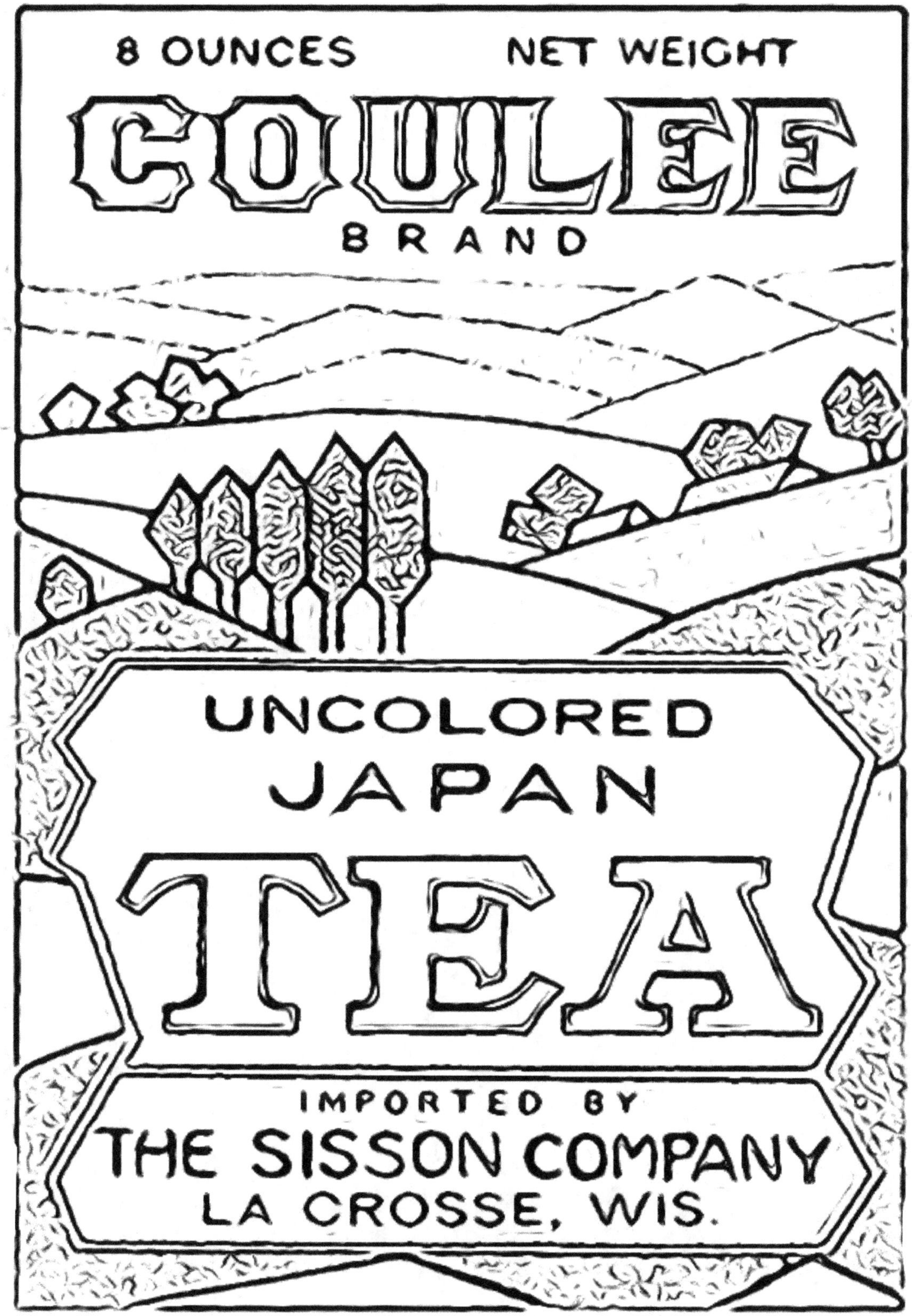

8 OUNCES   NET WEIGHT
COULEE
BRAND
UNCOLORED
JAPAN
TEA
IMPORTED BY
THE SISSON COMPANY
LA CROSSE, WIS.

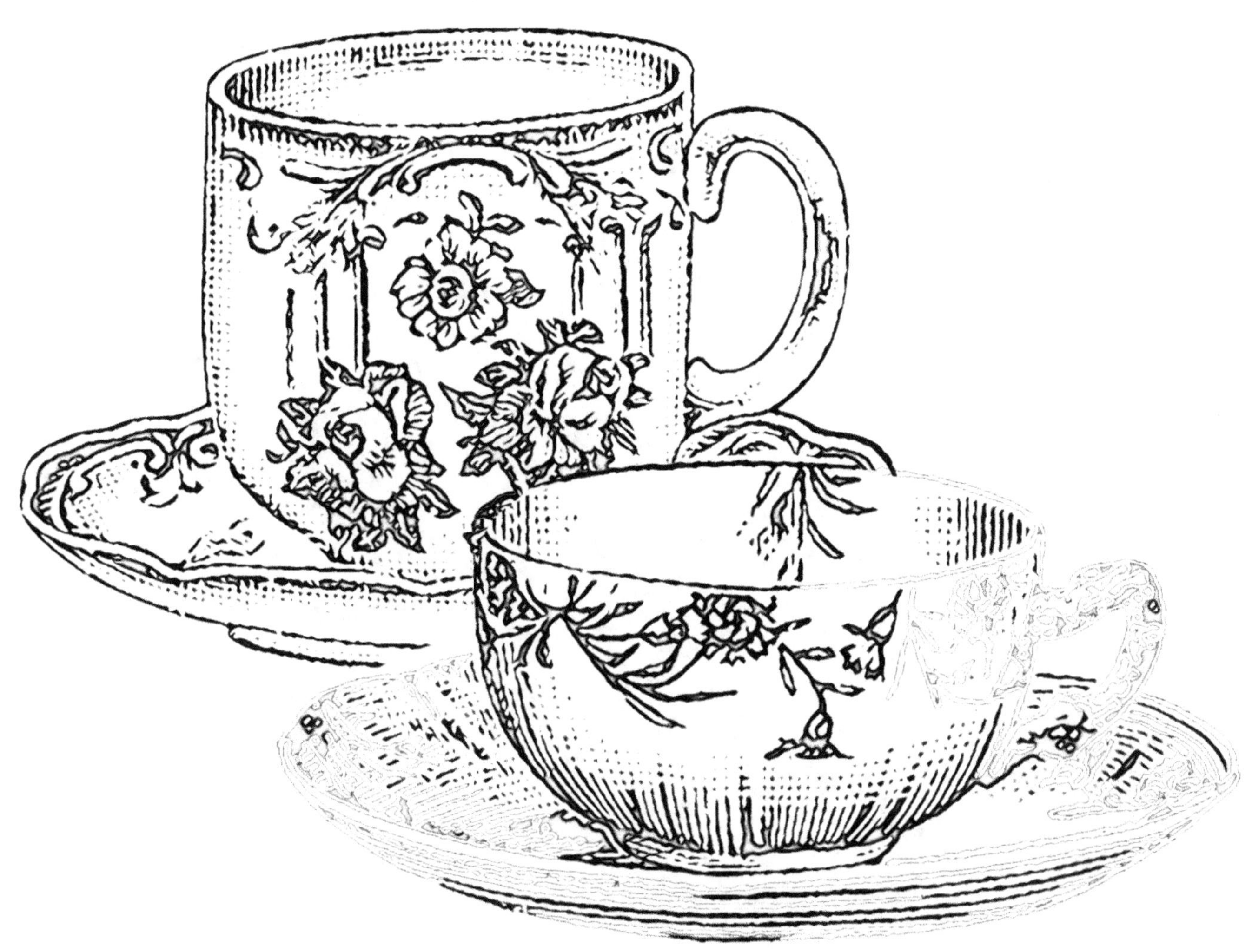

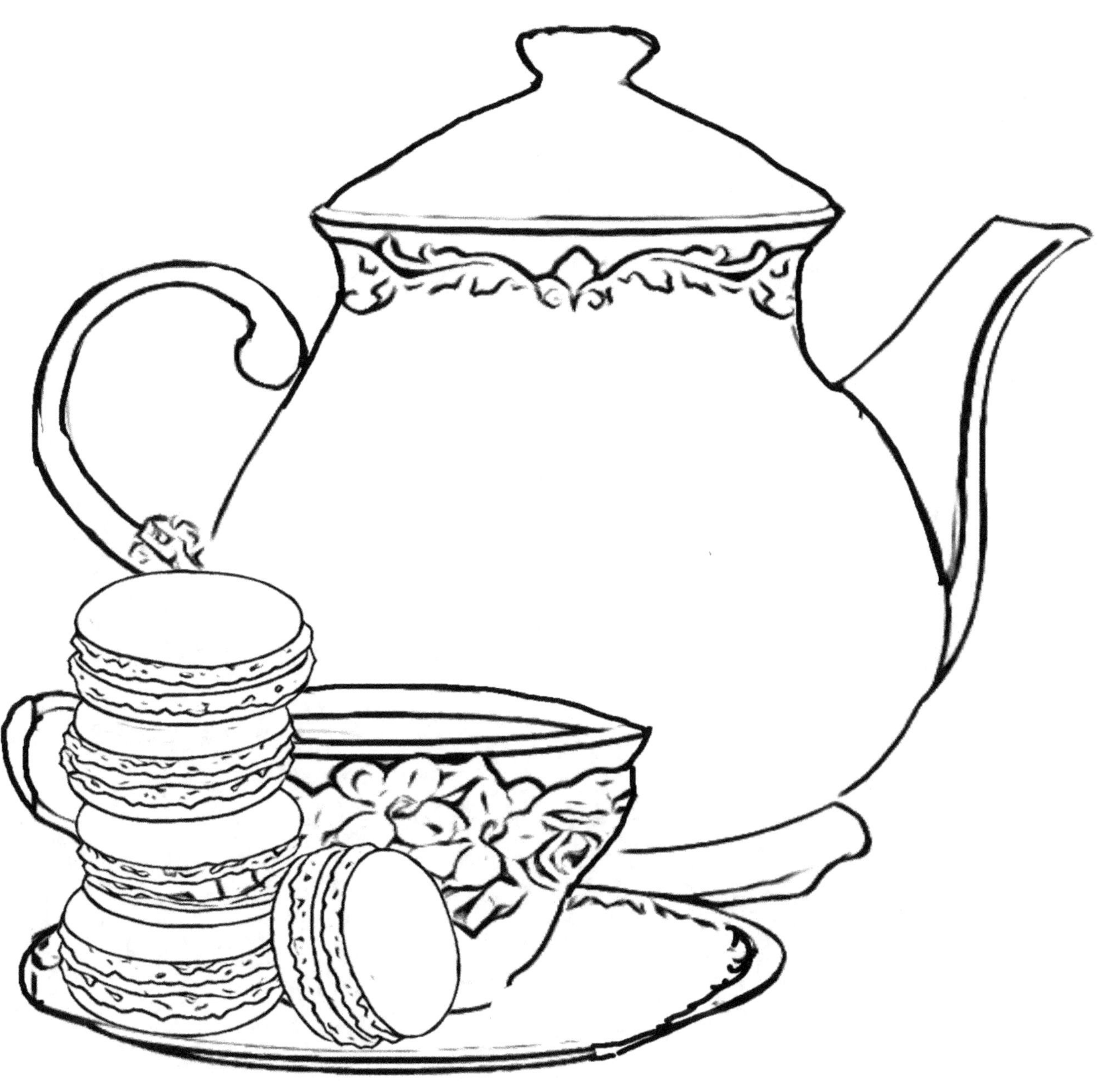

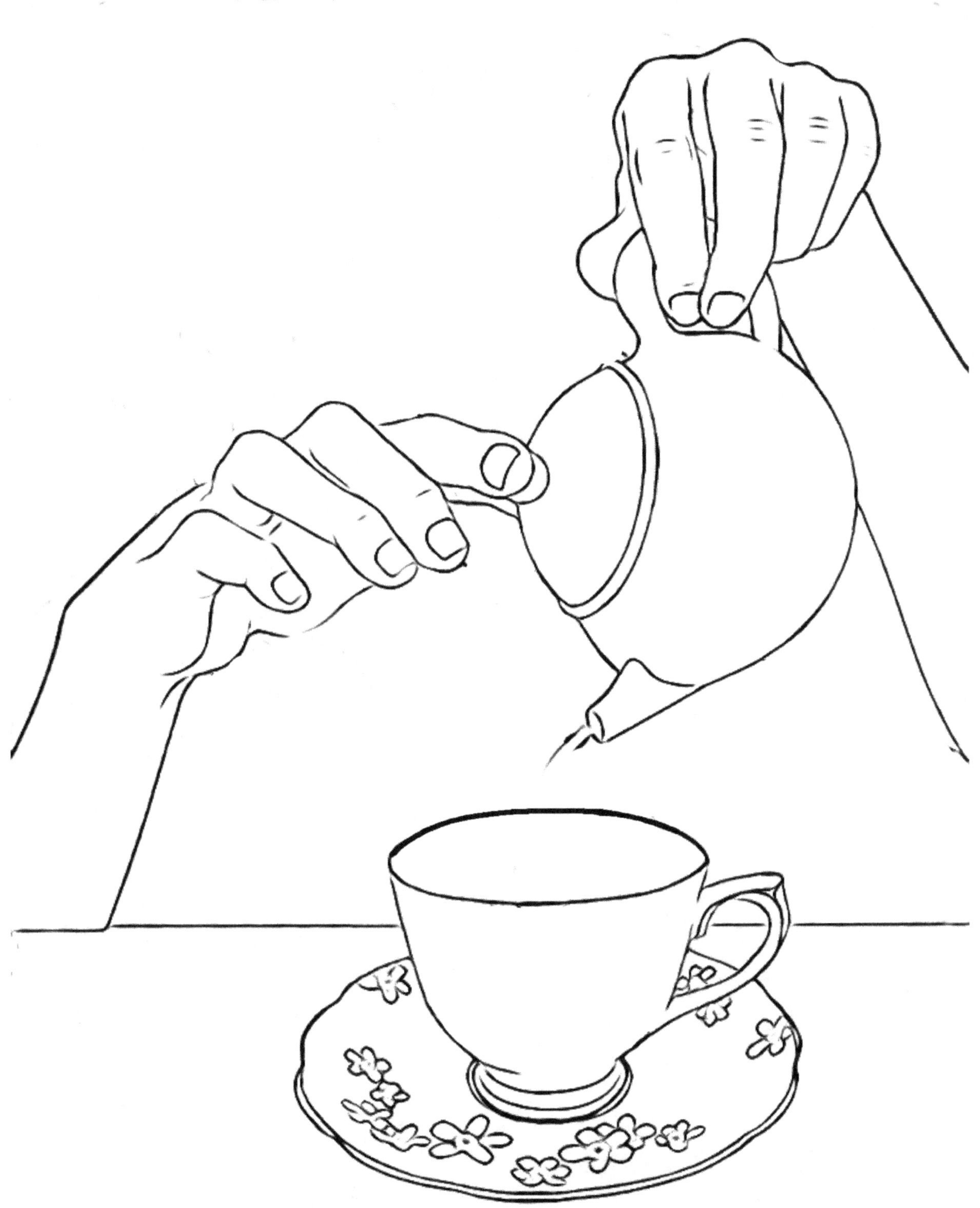

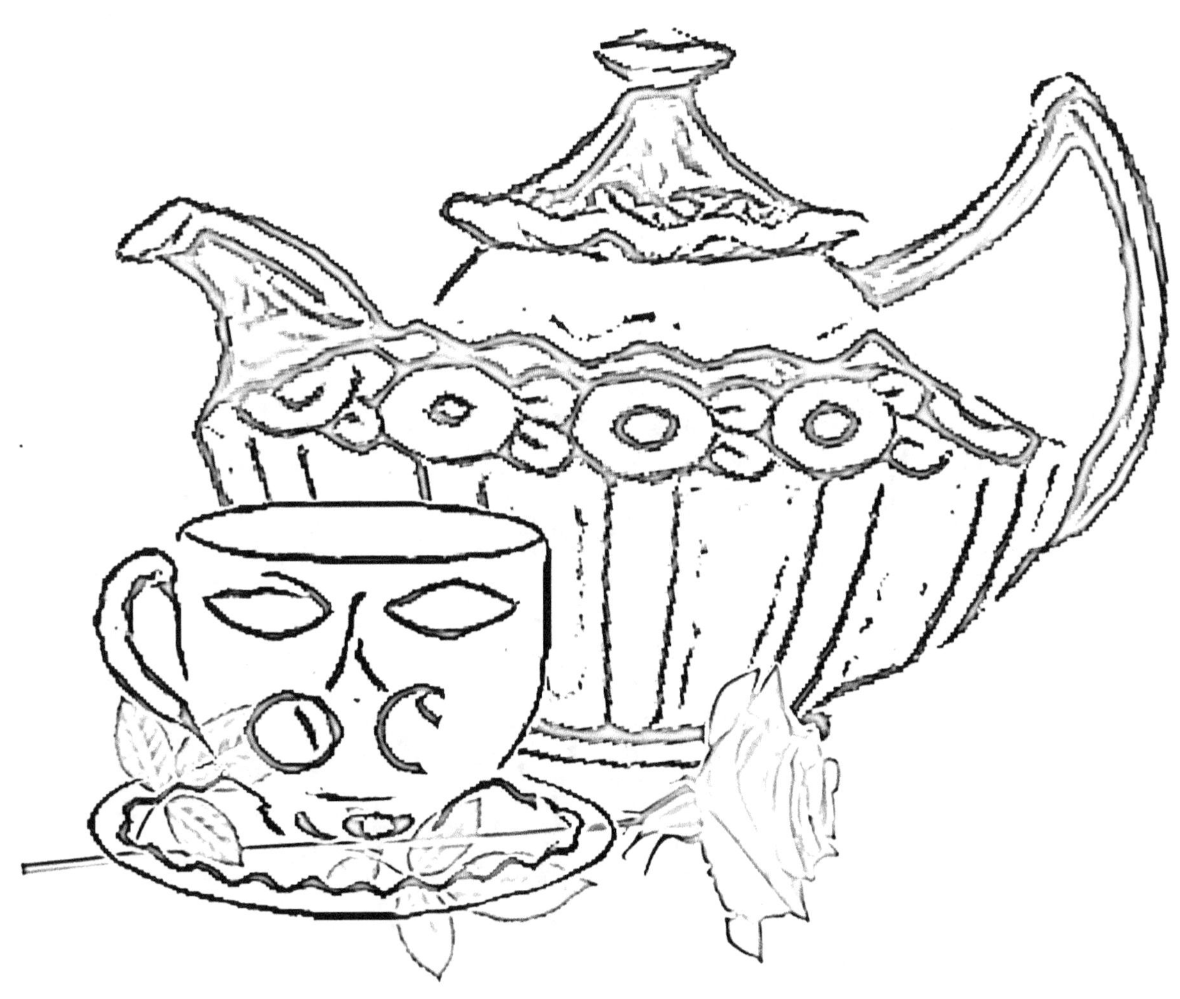

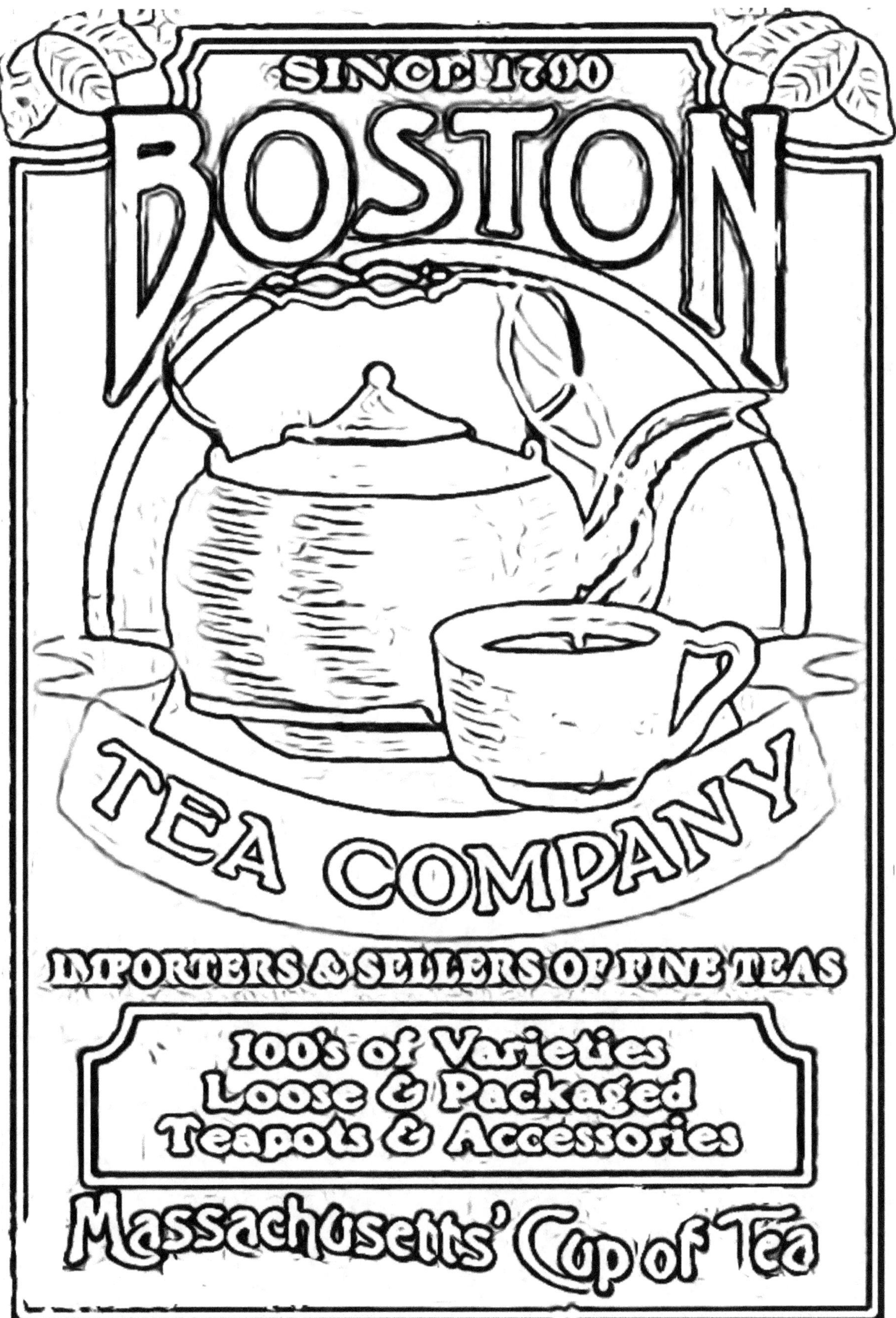

SINCE 1700
BOSTON
TEA COMPANY
IMPORTERS & SELLERS OF FINE TEAS
100's of Varieties
Loose & Packaged
Teapots & Accessories
Massachusetts' Cup of Tea

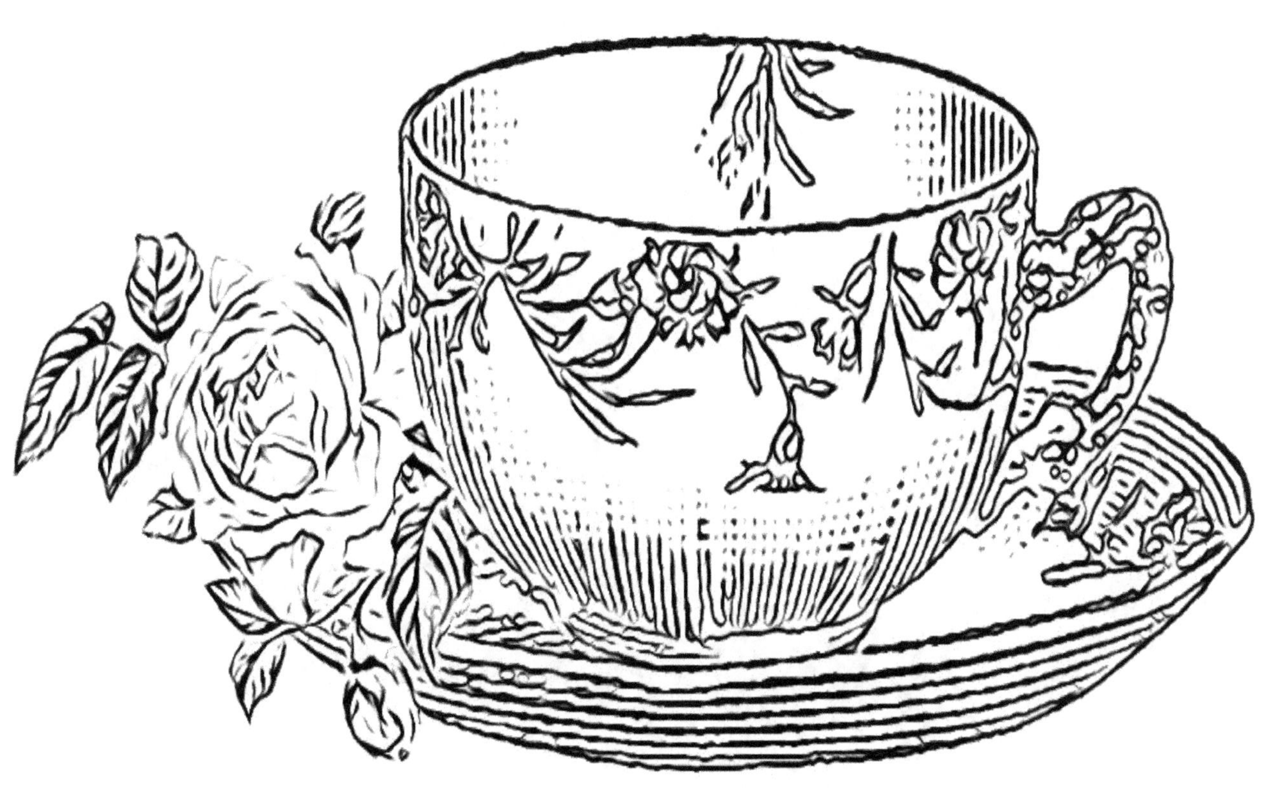

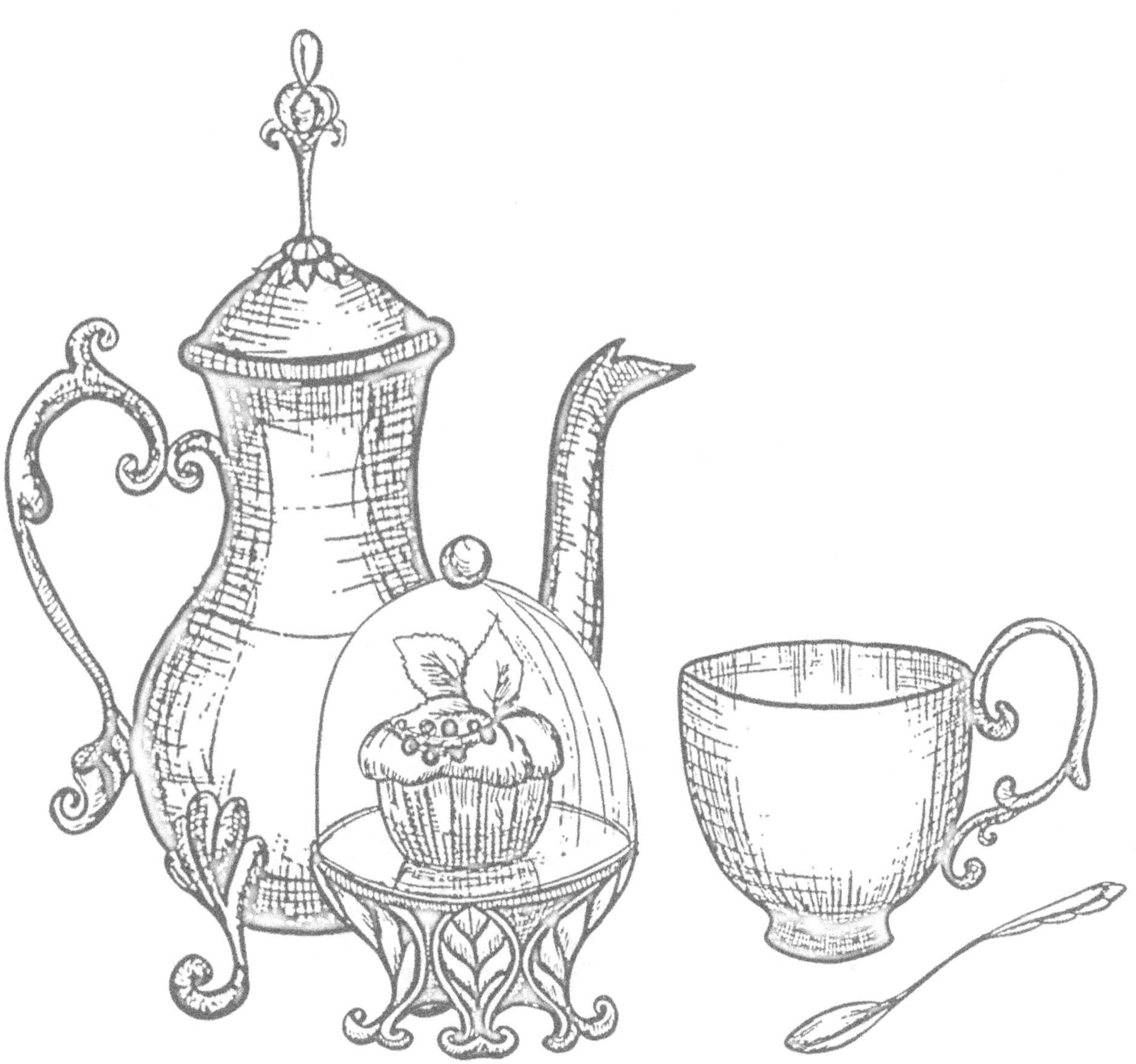

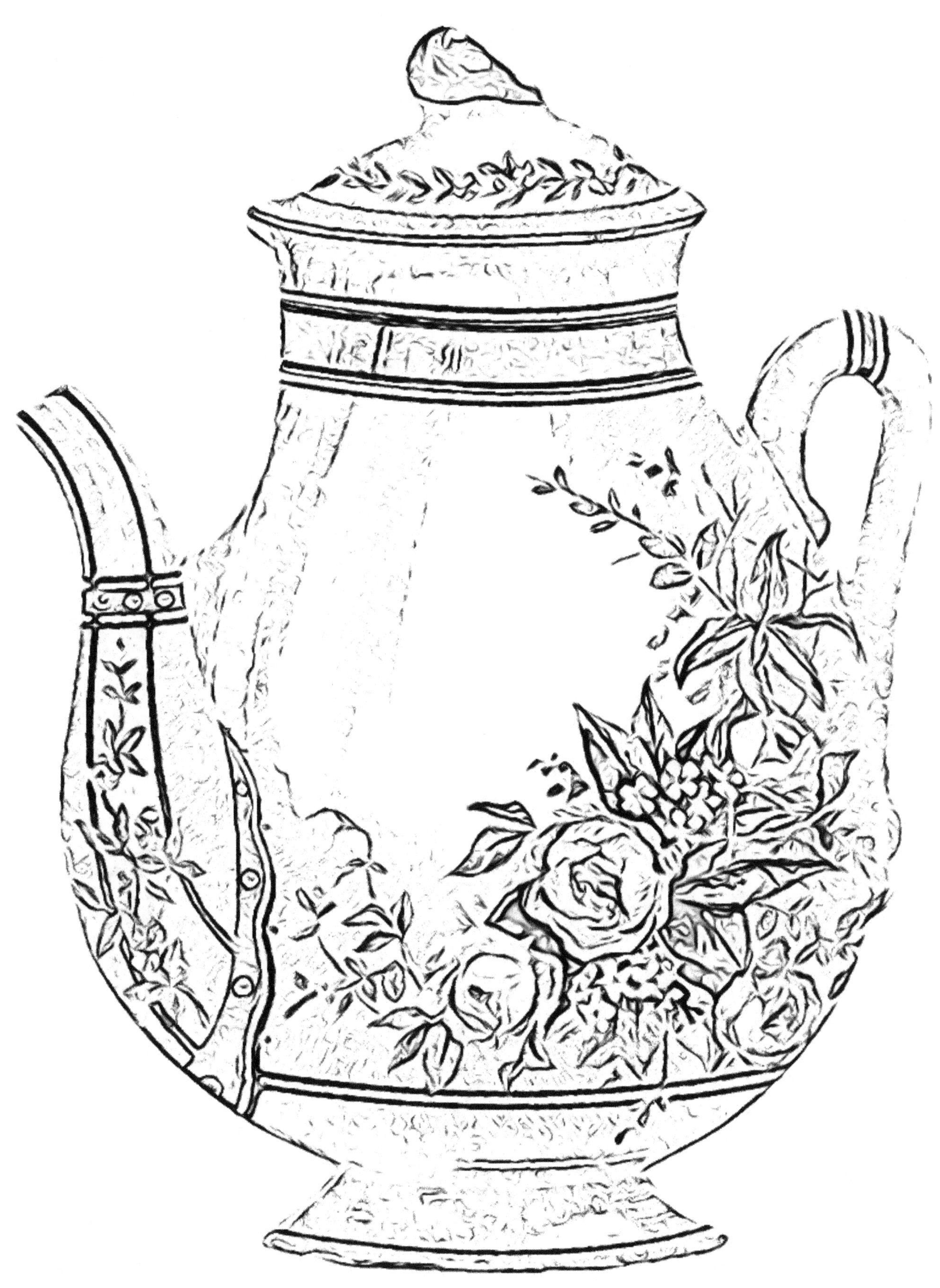

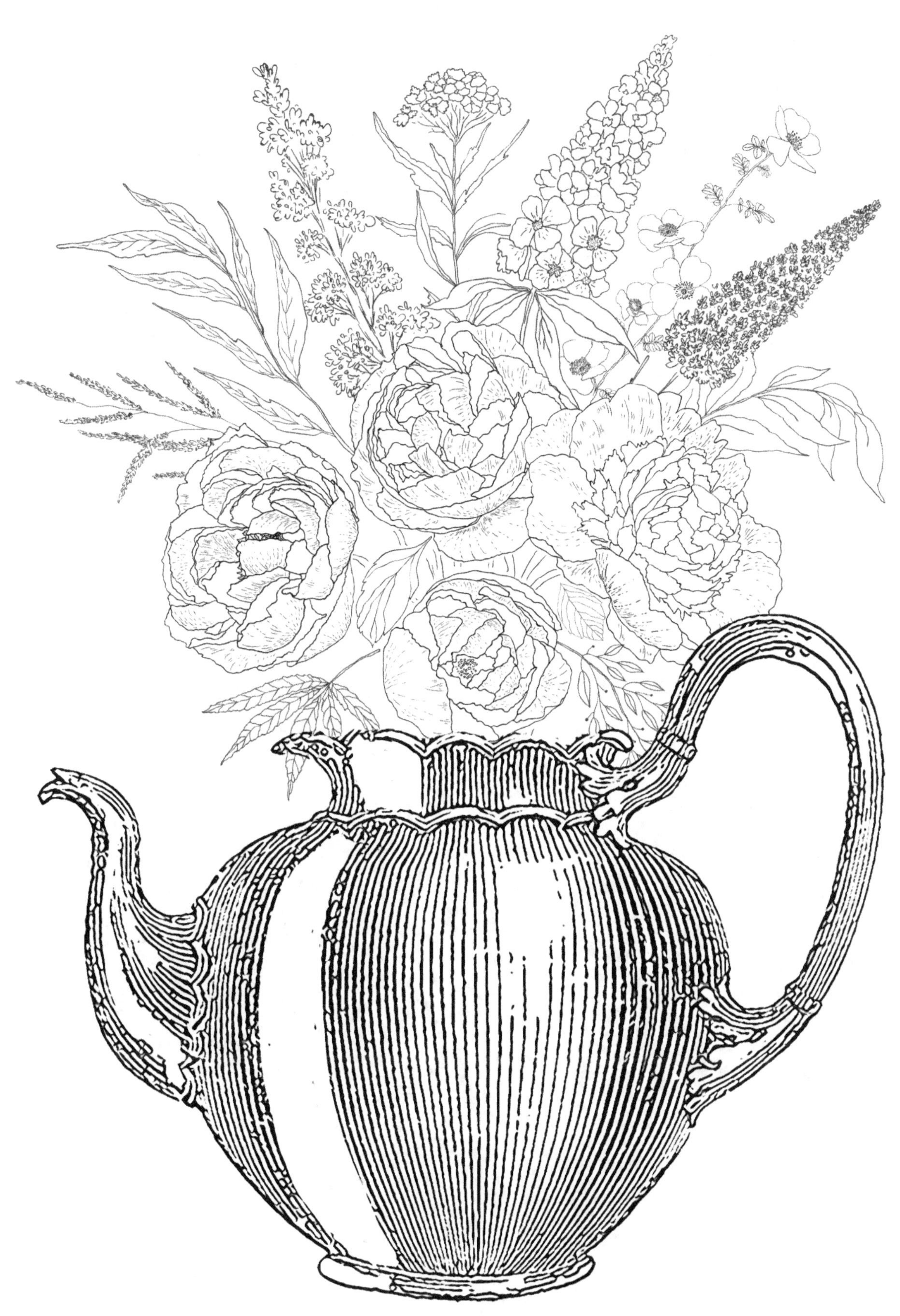

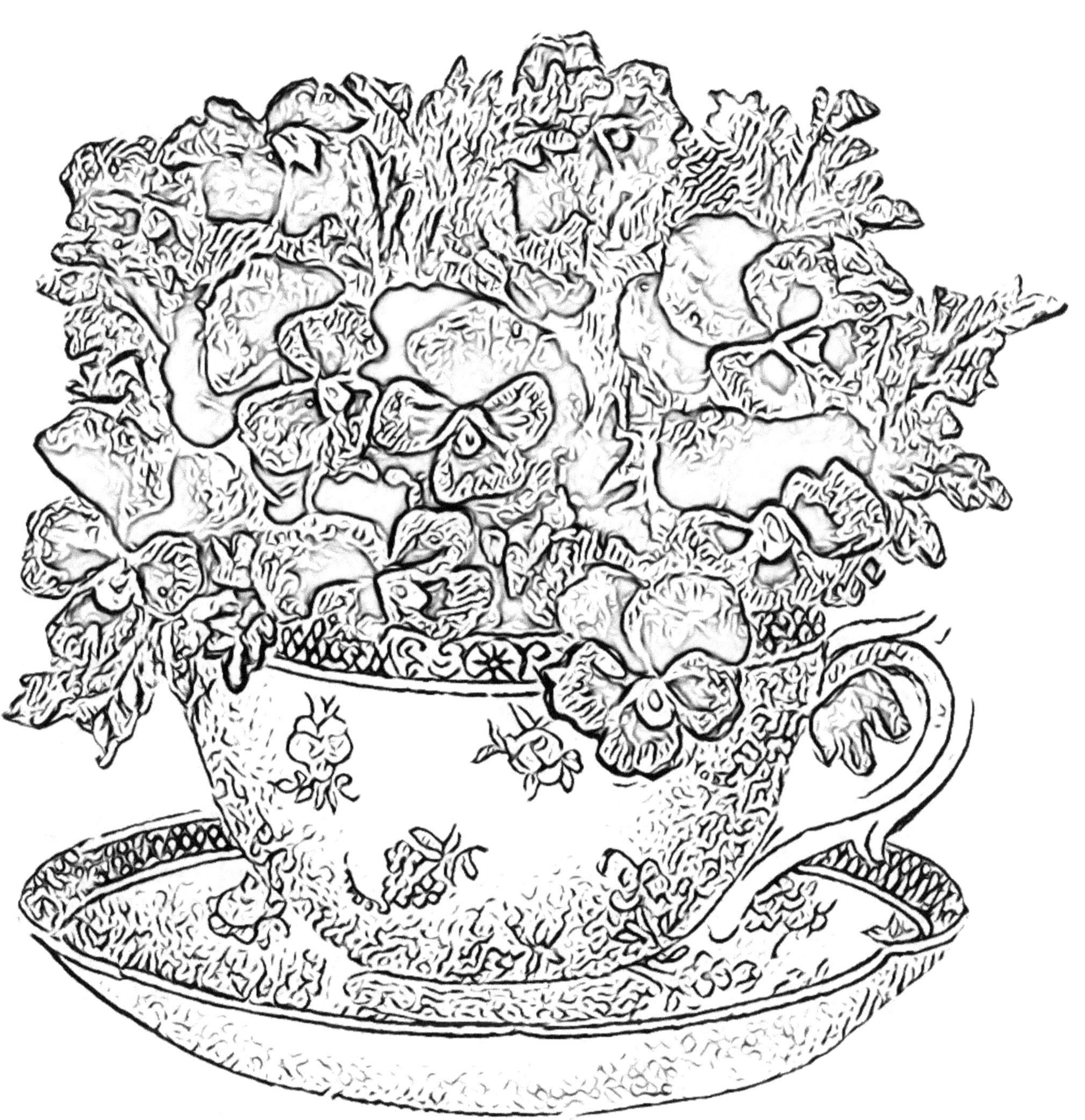

Also by Color me Vintage:

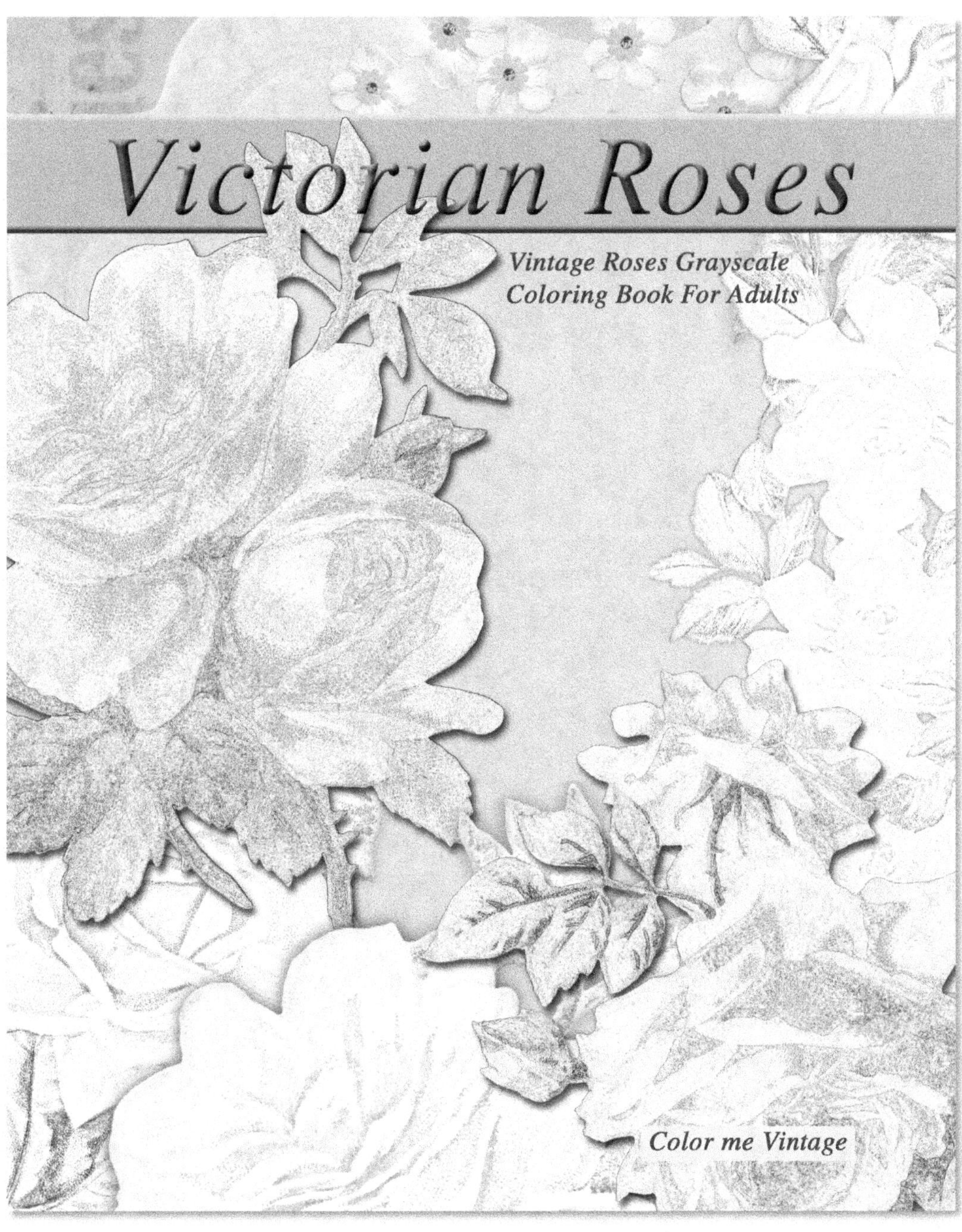